Taking My Time

Jan Norman
Taking My Time

For Asti
with thanks

Taking My Time
ISBN 978 1 76041 446 7
Copyright © text Jan Norman 2017
Cover image: Clocks on blue © Stillfx

First published 2017 by
Ginninderra Press
PO Box 3461 Port Adelaide 5015 Australia
www.ginninderrapress.com.au

Contents

The Future Imagined	7
Arrival	8
Getting the Ration Books	9
Summer – Memories of Childhood	11
Nice Girls Don't	13
Contradicting John Donne	15
No Poppies for Miss Hadley	16
The Beach	17
Searching for B	19
Ebb Tide of Communication	21
Apart	23
Reduction	24
The Milky Way	25
Day's end by the river	26
The Measure of the Year	27
Lines Written After Catching a Trout	28
Little Brown Bird	29
Mourning	30
Autumn Evening	31
Home Thoughts From Abroad	32
On Watership Down	34
Summer's End	35
Farewell Summer	36
Poem in Exile	37
Noontide	39
An Official Life	40
Face Value	41
The Plea	43
Call Back Yesterday	44
Brandy Beans	46

Identity	47
Prisoner of Expectation	48
Black is the night…	49
In Gratitude to Bruckner	50
Marlborough	51
Autumn	52
From the Summer House	53
Now	55
Lacrimae	56
After the Rain	57
Countryside in Winter	58
Parting	60
Retrospection	61
Poem for Richard	62
In Responsum	64
Small Town in the Morning	65
Hidden	67
Water	68
Listening	69
The General	70
Understood	71
The Long-case Clock	72
Runaway	73
Carpe Diem	74
What Did They Call Them?	75
A Rueful Lament	77
Thoughts on Pride and Prejudice	78
The Moggy's Revenge	79
The Day After	81
Requiem for a Foolhardy *Pholcus Phalangoides*	82

The Future Imagined

When I am grown old
will I still remember Me?
When I walk with care
down every stair,
will I still remember
dancing free?
When I sit and I nap
with a cat on my lap,
will I still remember
a lover – or three?
The adventures I had?
The friends, good and bad?
Will I reach out at all
towards memory's glass wall
and try to make contact with Me?

Arrival

You are,
You were,
You will be –
Decline the verb 'to be'?
Decline it not.
Rather rejoice
And so rejoicing rise
From brilliant agony
Alive; immortal
In your eyes
And greet the world
With these first frantic cries.

Getting the Ration Books

The news came rolling
Through the valleys
But the mountains fled,
Blue and quivering,
Into the distant mists.
'What's a war, Mummy?'
I wore my red dress,
She wore her blue
With the white flowers.
It was my favourite.
Grown-ups, very tall,
All legs and trousers,
Skirts flapping in my face,
Waited uncertain
In summer sunshine.
'What's a war, Mummy?'
'I'm worn out!' she gasped.
Seizing my hand, Nanna
trotted me down the path
From the RSL clubhouse
In shabby Lurline Street,
Onto the pavement
Sprouting clover and lolly papers.
She sat on the wall.
I looked up at the stones,
Rough and grooved
With sparkles in them
Where the sun struck.

I picked at the biggest sparkle
And it disappeared –
But my hand was empty.
I searched at my feet –
Cigarette ends, orange peel,
Papers, wooden ice cream
Spoons like dirty paddles –
Disappointment stung.
'Want to walk along the wall?'
Nan forestalled my whingeing,
Lifting me up so high
That I clung to her hand,
Full of fear and excitement.
So high in the world –
Higher than legs and skirts.
I could see people's faces!
Mummy waved from
The door with the wobbly sign.
She'd told me it said,
'RATION BOOKS HERE.'
Boldness grew in the sun
And I shouted, 'Hey!
Look at me! I'm big!'
And the mountains,
Ashamed of their fear,
Came out of the mists
Into the sunlight.

Summer – Memories of Childhood

Lying in my childhood's room,
I woke to the tenant sparrows
Gossiping in the honeysuckle on the fence;
Listened again to the sea surge
Striking the sandstone cliffs,
Booming a dull counterpoint
To the shrillness outside.
Through the open window drifted
The scent of hot, dry grass
Spiced with salt from the spray
Which dulled the mirrors
And the sun-washed glass.
Had so many years really passed
Since I'd smelled the heady frangipani
By the squeaking, green front gate;
Climbed the low, forbidden cliffs
From the searing, sun-hot rocks;
Swum with anxious eye out
For cruising sharks offshore
And for sea urchins lurking hidden
Underneath our wary feet?
We ate faintly gritty picnics then
When watermelon oozed, sweet and sticky,
Down salty, sunburned chins.
We used to have great family days
At Coal and Candle Creek and Kurrajong
Or Oyster Bay and sometimes,
All the way to National Park;
Singing our merry way there,
Squabbling our weary way home.

Now, so far away from childhood
And those hot, remembered days,
The sound of chirping sparrows
And the scent of dry, hot grass
Make me lift my head in query
And think I can…I'm sure I can…
Smell the sea – can't you?
Surely it is only over there,
Behind the ridge, just out of view?

Nice Girls Don't

The first time they said it
I was only seven,
A bouncy, chin-up,
Hands-on-hips, look-the-world-
In-the-face kind of kid,
Elbows out to get on the bus
With the high school giants
When it was squash or be squashed!
Someone reported the sight
To my grandmother.
'Nice girls don't do that.
They wait and take their turn.'
And get trampled on!
(No, she didn't say that. I did!)
When I was eight
I cried when I was pushed off
The seat in Musical Chairs.
Well, it was my birthday,
My party, my chairs.
(Well, ours anyway.)
'Nice girls don't cry
When they lose. They smile
And clap the winner.'
I tried to tell them
It was not losing but being pushed
To make me lose that upset me
But they seemed to hear
A different language.
I was less bouncy now.

'Nice girls don't sprawl.'
'Nice girls don't run
And leap for joy out in the street.'
'Nice girls wear hats and gloves
To go into town on the bus.'
'Nice girls don't wear trousers
On a hike when they have to
Go through the city en route.'
I had no bounce at all now
And looked at the world sideways.
After all, I wasn't a nice girl.
I had been told often enough
By people who ought to know
So I knew it had to be true.
In the end, I lived my real life
Inside my skull and performed
The pantomime of approved living.
And if occasionally
My chin strayed upwards
Or a trace of bounce was seen,
There was always someone there
To say, 'Nice girls don't.'

Contradicting John Donne

'No man is an island.'
Perhaps in Donne's context
but not in mine.
I am an island
alone in a sea of faces,
an ocean of noise
and news and nothingness.
I build bridges
round my coastline
to other islands,
each also alone
in its little space.
Fragile bridges break
like filaments of web
in the first storm;
sturdy ones endure
but need care and repair
when cracks appear.
Do I like my island state?
I know no other.
It has been so since childhood.
I tried: so often tried
to be part
of a continent of beings
who knew a world
I never found
or understood;
now at least
I've learned the art
of building bridges.
I guess I've become
an engineer of sorts!

No Poppies for Miss Hadley

Poppies flutter; brave blood-red flags
among the white reminders of the dead;
light and shadow in endless rows
where once the dead while living fought
and fell, entombed in mud with foe and friend,
all far from home in a foreign land.
Poppies in wreaths, man-made, constrained,
echo the field flowers in a ravished earth,
staining memorials of weathered stone
with shocking brightness in November's gloom.
There'll be no poppies for Miss Hadley, though.
Armistice did not bring her love's return.
Deprived of future husband, children, home;
holding memories pressed in her mind
like faded flowers, fragile and scentless,
her life slid by. Unremarkable, dowdy, plain;
a butt of ignorant schoolgirls' cruel jokes,
she taught me the language of the battle zone.
Le soldat, la guerre, la mort!
I hadn't noticed the tiny diamond glimmering
on her left hand or the locket always worn.
Late one day I found her weeping
in our hushed and empty classroom,
crawling on lisle-clad knees across the floor,
glasses awry, searching with shaking hands
for the ring made more precious by memory.
Silent, abashed by sorrow I did not comprehend,
I searched beside her, afraid to comfort
and enter that forbidden No-Man's-Land of grief.

On Remembrance Day there'll be no poppies
for the women who lost the lives they might have led
but I'll remember you, Miss Hadley. I'll remember.

The Beach

Beach curving to embrace an olive sea
White-lipped and warm,
Firm sand damp under bare feet;
Gaunt, windswept trees
Lean across the dunes
Above grey tussocks of harsh grass.
Behind the offshore islands,
Dull and shadowy
Yet vibrant with seabirds,
Storm clouds roll and gather.
He stands, breath held, remembering
Just such a long-ago day, when,
White dress fluttering in the wind,
The girl stood
Holding out a hesitant hand.
A wondering smile trembled,
Slipped away before his intent eyes,
While behind them the storm cloud rose
To surge across the sun
And leave them in the shadow of its coming.
Enrapt and still, they stood for a timeless moment
Knowing nothing but each other,
Till the first great drops of rain
Fell cold upon them
And they ran, laughing, hand in hand –
Two carefree children on a desolate shore…
He sighs and turns away
To find her standing – smiling.
Almost with surprise
He sees her there.

They smile again,
The wonder stolen by the years
And their footsteps trail more slowly
Over the ever-encroaching dunes.

Searching for B

I struggled, fought for life,
light, breath; arrived searching.
She looked, frowned, turned
aside, disappointed.
No pink and white doll to play with.
Wept, 'She looks like a plucked chook!'
I followed her through our days,
always behind, trailing,
calling, 'Wait for me. Stay with me.'
She hid before I could find her;
hid behind a screen of years,
of sulphur fumes in the nightmare
dark when her asthma struck;
behind homework and books,
behind friends. 'What a pest!'
They said but she frowned,
shrugged, looked sideways
at the small albatross
hanging around them, smiling up, hoping.
Too soon. She turned away,
following lectures, work, boyfriend.
Sometimes she called back to me
and her words floated past
while I leaped to catch them.
Sometimes they flew like darts
and lodged to fester in hidden places.

When she married, left home,
I was stranded on a dark platform.
The train had departed and I
had missed it; missed her.
I caught a later train and
found my sister, finally waiting
for me. She took my hand
and we walked forward together.

Ebb Tide of Communication

'What've we come here for, eh?
We must've been mad!'

>The empty beach spreads
>Its curving arms along the shore.
>See how the banyans bend above it
>In mute homage to the power beyond.
>Waves, carved from translucent jade,
>Break into fragments and die,
>Whispering a soft lament upon the sand.

'God, what a dead hole! Nothing to see –
I'll bet there's not a decent restaurant here.
Nothing but…'

>Miles of loneliness
>And strutting sea gulls
>Printing stiff red feet
>In tide-wet, rippled sand
>Pockmarked with bubbles.
>Waves fling white-encrusted
>Droplets at the sun
>To hang, shot with colour,
>Against the infinite blue.

'…bloody sea and sand.
What'll we do, for Christ's sake?'

> I shall run like a child
> Through the warm, lilting shallows,
> Splashing and laughing in the sunlight.
> I shall lift my arms to the sun
> And embrace the moment,
> Remembering I am alive.
> I shall let the sand run through my fingers,
> Warm and dry, soft and caressing
> Upon my bare thighs.
> I shall find myself – alone.

'What are you smiling for?
I don't know why you're always smiling to yourself –
You never tell me what you're thinking…
If it's anything at all.
It probably isn't worth hearing anyway!'

> The sea is calling;
> its roar demanding,
> Its murmuring a plea.
> I'm listening – I'm coming…
> Wait for me…wait for me…

Apart

The sadness
and hurt cried out
from his white face
and stricken eyes,
and from mine.
I wanted to hold out
forgiving arms
and give comfort
but there was no comfort
in me for him
and none in him
for me.
I could only stand
apart
while my heart
wept in pity
for our loneliness.

Reduction

I lived only
in the present.
Now
was that moment, that breath.
I closed my mind to the past.
I dared not look beyond
the room
which shrank around me
as the moment shrank;
my world
reduced to that chair
on which I sat;
nothing left but body,
nothing left but mind.
I was my world.

The Milky Way

Star-bright river
spreads across the meadows
of the dark night sky.
I dream of boating,
floating, buoyed
by the moonlight,
drifting on through
its glittering shoals,
till silvered with stardust
I slip through its shallows,
down into daybreak,
down into dream-fade.

Day's end by the river

Distant frog call breaking stillness
Old when giant gums were grass high;
Trembling water moves reflections,
Bending telegraph-trunks at will,
Dragging clouds like fresh-shorn fleeces
Far into its green-black depths,
There to quiver, trapped and fading
as the dark replaces light;
Nothing heard but water whispering,
Veiling willow-hidden rocks;
All half-seen, no glint of moonlight –
Yet shadow birds swoop darkly by.

The Measure of the Year

>   …ice whispers.

Earth beats, heart beats;
Laughter and sunlight
Growing together.

Porcelain flowers,
Myriad petals floating.
Hidden fragrance.

Golden children
Poised on the curving dunes.
Sea hawk gliding.

Ripening grain bends
Performing obeisance to the sun
Before the sacrifice.

Rain drifting,
Washing the face of the morning.
Shrouded sunlight.

Firelight –
Wraithlike shadows dancing.
Leaves on the wind.

Glittering branches,
Shadows against a saffron sky.
Wood smoke rising.

Monochrome landscape
Frozen into lifeless silence.
Unquiet ice whispers.

Earth beats…

Lines Written After Catching a Trout

Slender line trailing,
Lost in green depths
Unknown world away.

Tautening suddenly,
Vivid life thrashing,
Lured by the metal fish.

Panic-drawn line up,
Prism lights blotted out,
Gravel and sand-torn.

Gasping in anguish,
Snatched from a vibrant life
Deep in the river –

Part of the flowing mass;
Light in its flickering lights,
Dark in its shadow weeds.

Weeping and guilty
Giving him back
To the river's embrace.

Little Brown Bird

in memory of my mother

Little brown bird
Where have you flown?
The skies are empty,
A breeze gently stirs
The bright leaves
Of spring
While cats doze
Under the lilac
And golden bees hum
Their timeless tune
In the lavender's mist.
Little brown bird,
There is no one now
To sing to me the song
Which you alone could sing.
The shadows lengthen
Hour by hour;
Perhaps in the cool dusk
Which marks the end
Of all our days,
I shall hear again
The flutter of wings,
Your song of love –
And I shall be content.

Mourning

Tattered clouds drift,
grey shadows
over the empty moon.
Winter's sigh
rustles dead leaves
gathered into shoals
on the frost-bleached grass.
A pattern of leaf shadows
moves across my face
in the cold light.
I stand alone
imprisoned in memories,
while around me
light and air are moving
yet unmoved
by the manner of her going
or by my sorrow.

Autumn Evening

The sun
from its receding fastness
caressed my grateful back
with its sensuous warmth
and murmured tales
of summer past.
On my face
the breeze, chill
from the first snow
on the distant mountains,
whispered of unfriendly winter
still to come.
At my feet
by the garden's edge,
a cricket crouched,
half-hidden
by slender grass shadows
and made the long stems
tremble with its song.
High above,
in the naked sky,
a hawk hovered,
patient in its hunger,
a tiny shadow on the hill.
It dived
and I was glad
I could not hear
the anguished cry
from its helpless prey
farewelling its too-brief life –
and that remembered day.

Home Thoughts From Abroad

England in April, revealing beauty here
To delight my senses but not my homesick heart
Which remembers still the land left long ago,
Far from this flowering, scented place;
Beyond oceans; beyond time and space.
There, golden birch and shimmering poplars grow,
Spendthrift intruders from this northern land.
Amidst the blue-green haze of eucalyptus-scented trees,
They toss their bright unwanted riches
Onto the thirsty, scarcely-flowing stream
Dreaming of winter's turbulent rains
But creeping, lethargic still and quiet
Far below, between
Red-ochre cliffs, unseen.
There, lyre birds dance and currawongs
Fling their rippling carols to the sun
While wing-still cicadas sleep,
Silent now, their summer song long gone,
In autumn's heat-forgotten chill.
Through the clear air, the unfolding hills
Rise, carved from lapis, with amethyst beyond.
Above them, a drifting eagle, solitary and free,
In lazy, graceful arcs on cushioning air
Surveys the forest and fern-shaded creeks
Where bellbirds monotonously chime
The hours of present, past and future time.

There, children grow unseen and smile
At other faces; mine is absent still –
And friends who meet, do they remember me
Except in passing, fleetingly
At festivals once shared?
All that was familiar is familiar still to them
While memory-racked I stand
In this familiar, distant land.
And yet, if I once more gladly walked
Along those far-off, distant shores,
I wonder if some contrary part of me
Would turn to wistful thoughts of England there
And its singing, April-scented air?

On Watership Down

High on the downs
Kites and castles in the air
And the cloud shadows running:
Over the burnished fields below
The brown fog comes oozing
Obscenely swallowing the bright world.
High on the downs
Where the larks rejoice,
Spiralling, soaring,
Bringing life to the empty sky,
I look to the south
Where the sun still shines,
Till storm clouds rise, rapidly
Obscuring the brightness.
Hostile black arms outstretch
And reach towards me
So that I turn away
From the frosted radiance
Behind their thunder
And the faint flicker
Of lightning at their heart;
Turn away
From the larks and drifting kites
And with coward feet
Hasten down,
Knowing the taste of fear
Amidst the sweet scent
Of fresh-cut hay and hedgerow flowers.

Summer's End

As summer fades
like dreaming
and autumn blows
back into our lives
on the north-east wind,
then leaves like flames
burn the shadows
in the dry, bleached grass.

As summer fades
like mist at daybreak
and autumn plucks
the sun-ripe seeds,
they scatter; hide
like wilful children
to surprise us
in the distant spring.

Farewell Summer

Farewell summer.
When those we see
as young are old,
your long, hot days
will be remembered
like those other rare
hot brilliant seasons,
sadly few among so many
that were grey and chill.
You were a summer
to celebrate,
your sunlit days
of blue and gold
made us walk
more lightly
through our lives,
laugh more gaily,
rest more quietly,
feel ourselves renewed.
Farewell summer.
I grieve to see you go.
Through the long, dark days
which lie ahead,
I'll watch and hope
for your return.

Poem in Exile

Rain flickers,
Windblown
Against the glass,

But there –
Does the heat
Still quiver
On the distant hills?

Early dusk
Hides
The huddling street,

But there –
Is the forest
Aflame
In the dying day?

Wind sighs,
Whispering
A winter's tale,

But there –
Do the great stars
Glitter
Above the firelight?

Is the river
Still whispering
Below the bluff?

Can you hear
The boobook's
Mournful cry?

Do the golden
Children
Dance still on the dunes?

Does the ochrous dust
Drift
Across the sun?

Oh tell me
Friend
Of my heart's home!

Noontide

The world is awash with light.
It brims over the rim of the sky
And pours through muslin clouds,
Trickles down mountains and skyscrapers,
Crashes against glaciers and windows,
Splashes on leaves and upturned eyes,
Squeezes through cracks in the barn
And round hostile, sentry curtains
To dance with dust motes.
Leaving its whitewashed spume
On the farmhouse walls
It ripples gently over the face
Of the blind man listening in vain
For the sound of its passing,
Feeling with outstretched hands
For the sparkle, the glitter,
The rainbow arabesques in the river.
Only the warmth cannot elude him
And he holds it hungrily
While the light flows on,
Flooding the stripped fields
Tawny after the harvest,
Till the tide is turned
By the afternoon shadows
Which lengthen and stretch,
Pushing it inexorably back
Towards tomorrow.

An Official Life

She was feisty
and young,
rebellious of
paternal control –
'unmanageable';
fell in love,
unsuitably
and didn't
countenance denial –
'promiscuous';
told her younger sister
about the facts
and joys of sex –
'depraved';
locked in the asylum,
unloved, neglected
for fifty long
corrosive years –
'incurable';
returned to uncare
in the community
even though
a half-century
of asylum
had stripped her sanity –
'progress';
died unregarded,
amidst the other litter
in the darkness
of an urban doorway –
'statistic'.

Face Value

I'm in disguise.
You don't know
Who I really am
Behind the mask of age.
The young dismiss
Grey hairs and lines
Of laughter or of grief;
Cannot believe that we
Have been where they are,
Have done it all before
And smile to see them
Discover our old world anew.
But in my secret world
Behind this screening face
I still walk barefoot
In seaside shallows;
Run through autumn mists
And kick the leaves
Which drift across the grass;
Send flat stones skimming,
Skipping on wavelets
On the village pond;
Climb trees and swing
From leaf-cloaked branches;
Turn handsprings on the lawn,
Scrump apples from their trees,
Pick bluebells in the woods.
I sing with the birds
And dance with the sun.

And yet, when young,
I was as blind as they
And did not understand
There is no time to kill –
Behind the mask of age
A child is laughing still.

The Plea

Do not end
day of dreaming,
filled with fragrance –
and I singing
with the day's song.
Do not slip
like water
through my hands
as night,
the servant of time,
drives you
beyond the hills,
beyond dreaming,
to leave me
mourning
in the unfriendly dark.

Call Back Yesterday

She drives through
the autumn countryside
dozing under its drift-leaf coverlet,
seeking the past;
half-afraid of remembering,
fearful of forgetting.
Suddenly she sees it.
The old house,
born of the Restoration –
an inviolable castle
to childhood's eyes –
stands now, gaunt and forgotten
in a sea of rampant grass,
thistles and dandelion
clocks which float away
on the wind, silver fragments
against the sun.
The tall windows, many-paned,
where once they stood to watch
the first snowfall of winter
spread its fragile mantle
over the summer-remembering garden,
are blind and empty,
haunted now by marauding birds
whose squabbling cries
resound through dusty rooms,
replacing the ghostly echoes
of their youthful voices.

Oh, house of distant childhood
and of dreams,
your glory and your ghosts
have blown away,
as ephemeral as dandelion clocks
on the chill wind of change.

Brandy Beans

Couched in their curving cradles
of shining, artificial brown,
they lie like newborn babies
swathed in chocolate bunny rugs
in some well-regimented nursery.
Ignoring cannibalistic overtones
I place one on my eager tongue,
tingling with greedy anticipation
and with a decisive crunch
release the imprisoned liquor
from its protective capsule,
feeling it trickle deliciously
around my receptive mouth.
And as I flick a fugitive drop
of sweetness back into warm darkness
and the scent of exotic cocoa oils,
I stare into the haunted chasms of the fire
where flames flicker-licker silently
and the fragrant woodsmoke
beguiles the midnight air.

Identity

Daughter, sister, cousin, aunt,
lover, wife and friend.
Am I a closet thespian
playing many roles?
Or just a ragbag
of personalities?
Identity in the eye
of the beholder, perhaps?
Novelist, poet, painter –
spear-carrying roles
at present but –
who knows?
If only I could find
just one real me,
a core immutable,
round which
these characters revolve.
Am I just a kaleidoscope
where shards of glass
make bright, changing patterns
but have no lasting form?
Australian? British?
In each of my countries
I defend the other, so –
nationality unresolved.
Perhaps I'm just a chameleon
and my real identity
is hidden –
even from myself.

Prisoner of Expectation

'Ought' and 'Should' –
I've let you rule my life.
The chains of expectation
chafe my ageing flesh
and it's too late
to call the blacksmith
and have him hew
those rusty links apart,
but if when young
I'd flung my chains
to fly in clinking arcs
into oblivion –
what could I have become?

Black is the night…

Black is the night
behind the glass
which mirrors
the familiar room.
Turn off the light.
We'll slip outside
where restless leaves
command our silence –
sssh…sssh…sssh.
Looking around
with light-drowned eyes,
resuscitation is swift
as pupils stretch
to draw in starlight.
A pale hanging moon
reaches down to send
leaf shadows quivering
across the spangled grass.
Myriad rain pools,
like studio monitors,
each with its miniature moon,
are banked, remote-controlled,
across the drive.
Ears rested by silence
can faintly hear
the singing of the bats,
passing more swiftly
than eye-blink.
Turn off the light.
Rediscover the forgotten
world of night.

In Gratitude to Bruckner

Brave trumpets blow
and hold the enemy at bay
beyond the shining glass
in a world grown grey,
where the unfriendly wind
sends brown leaves scurrying,
showers impotent raindrops
and rolls them, hurrying
in frantic rivulets
which meet and meeting, blend –
chilled but not by loneliness,
knowing none and seeking no friend.

Blow trumpets; bravely
keep loneliness at bay.
Your music fills the silence
of this slow, quiet day.

Marlborough

Above,
a silver-winged bullet scores
a long, white furrow
across the wakening sky.
From behind the mist,
the sun reaches out
to touch the crests
of the hills
and wipe away
the shadows of the night.
The church clock
strikes the hour.
Beneath
the vanishing shadows
a town emerges, stirs;
its eyes blink open
as curtains swish
and doorways gape and yawn.
Lighted windows show
a shadow play
of people's lives
as a country town
awakes.

Autumn

I heard autumn
speak to me
in the flutter
of the leaves
on the porch;
in the hard, high cry
of the birds,
blown about
the wind-stripped sky.
I heard it
in the chill wind
itself, shivering
the long grass
once summer-bright
then frost-faded.
The wind ruffled
the river,
black in the shadow
of the trees,
which floated the spent gold
of the bending poplars
in a ragged regatta
towards the falls.

From the Summer House

At the top of the garden
where the blackthorn blew
like spring snow in sunshine,
stood the summer house.
She opened the door, its faded timber
shrunk so that the south-west wind
entered without prior arrangement
through the uneven gaps.
She lifted the plastic sheeting
hung to repel such intrusion
and like the hermit crab
vulnerable without it,
slipped into this waiting shell.
Here in her own quiet place
she was not alone. The people
of her current imagining
were all around her.
From here she could see the world,
hear its voices, write its name.
Sometimes the guns boomed
from over the downs,
somewhere on Salisbury Plain
and she would look down
at the house she had left
and imagine a screaming missile
reducing it to broken bricks
and splintered wood
spiked with carpet shreds.

Books, released from their shelves,
would fly higher and farther
than their authors ever dreamed;
bricks, wood, carpet, books
impregnated with tension and shared pain,
with miscommunication and with fear.
Long silences and cold hostility
haunted the vaulted roof space
until her cathartic blast.
Afterwards she would remember
the warmth of that now-lost love
which had supported her,
been the deciding factor
in long-ago decisions
with unexpected consequences.
It too must have been absorbed
into the fabric of the house
and have been dissolved
by her reflective terrorism.
And then her other self,
whom she carried around
like a dead and decaying
Siamese twin, would revive
cry out in pain and speak
to overwhelm her,
not with the joy of restoration
but with an old, established grief.

Now

There is no future,
Only yesterday
And now – and now.
Sick with old pain
And raw foretelling
I hang on the wire
Between the abyss
Of yesterday
And the no-man's-land
Of tomorrow
Where dreams die –
Rat-a-tat-tat…
The Furies are firing.
How can I move
Except to go on
Hanging, swinging,
Feeling the cold wire
Hooked into my flesh?
I'm twisting, turning
As it wraps more tightly
Around raw wounds
Like screaming mouths.
Can you hear them, God?
They call on you.
Are you too distant,
Too busy with the universe
Going on and on,
Taking you farther away,
So that their cries
Are just pinpricks of sound
In the cosmic silence?

Lacrimae

The well of tears
is capped,
not dry.
I cannot drown
in old griefs
nor quench the new.
Memories spring
like weeds
but quickly die.
Despite repair,
through tiny cracks
the water weeps.
Scalding images
of pain and loss
and others' grief,
when those I watch
and I are one,
allow relief.

After the Rain

Raindrops,
captured by leaves
thirsty after drought,
are slowly released
to drop with slow, erratic
'plop' upon the path.
In the rose bed
bushes bend in grief
as perfumed petals,
cut from arching stems
by razor darts of rain,
lie prostrate
on the ground.
Mock orange, bridal white,
recoils from falling blossoms
ravished, dying
in the rain's last
furious assault.
Life-giver and destroyer,
the storm sweeps on.
Restored to power
the sun appears,
the dark earth steams
and sparrows chatter,
splashing wing-stretched
in the dying pools.

Countryside in Winter

Ancient chalk downland
Sweeps towards a grey-slate sky
Where raucous rooks swirl
Or float like charred leaves
From autumn's last bonfire.
Young beech trees,
Whispering secrets
Under their tawny cloaks,
Stand like poor monks
In the forest cathedral
Where bare twigs
And arching branches
Above tall slender trunks
Replace the soaring perpendicular.

Under the opaline ice
Of the deserted lake
Dark water waits,
Its life suspended
Till renascent spring.

In the bulging cottages
Strung like tattered onions
Along the old coach road,
Villagers huddle by fires
And sip gratefully
At hot tea or cocoa
Before reluctantly creeping
Up to icy bedrooms
Under the sprouting thatch.

The first snowflakes
Fall silently,
Unseen at midnight,
Speckling the church tower
Decorating tilting gravestones,
Lichened and anonymous,
With white ice-flowers,
While in the frozen ground
Old bones wait patiently still.

Parting

I know you've gone
but your jacket
seems to hold your shape.
I press my cheek
against its rough tweed;
your scent lingers there.
For a moment I can pretend
but – it's only a moment
and then…
I know you've gone.
Around me the silence swirls
as abrasive as sand;
my skin prickles at its touch,
my stretching ears listen, long
to hear your voice once more
saying…anything,
no matter how mundane,
I don't care – but nothing stirs
and then…
I know you've gone.
I wake at midnight.
Was it just a passing fox
and the wind
fading with the moonrise
or did I hear you cough and sigh?
And yet…
I know you've gone.
So is this pain I carry
your parting gift to me?

Retrospection

I sit among your possessions
and I wonder,
was I yet another
or did I possess your love
as you possessed mine?
It seemed so once
and then it changed.
I saw it in your eyes
and in the absence
of those same words
I spoke to you.
'What shall I do?'
I asked my mother,
so recently dead
and thought I heard her say,
'Be brave. All ends
one day – even pain.'
My love went on
as I did, though
more slowly
and when the end
arrived, I saw you smile
and your lips formed a kiss
which spoke the words
you could never say.
In gladness, I believed
yet sometimes though
I wonder – so I write
this poem to still
the questions in my heart.

Poem for Richard

He sits and reads,
wonders and remembers
fragments of a life;
searching in other lives,
other histories, other thoughts,
for links; connections
which will help him
understand his own.
Delving into poems,
he lives the pain
spilling from the page
in woven words
which the poet wraps
like a counterpane
around them both.
His memory
sends him postcards
from forgotten ports
in which, observant,
he wandered once,
when youth was now
and time-worn age
unplanned; unknown.

From thoughts
in other minds
to which he's linked
by their words and his,
he recreates his life;
distils impressions
onto a new, clean page,
makes sense and order
from a jumbled past.
His questing mind,
deprived of sustenance
by war, then work,
feasts now on words.
This third-age scholar
is a happy man.

In Responsum

Sensuous metaphors
entwine thoughts,
coming alive
to somersault
across the page,
conjuring delight.
Images float,
dissolve like mist
or cling to crags
of recognition.
Siren songs call
to my long-neglected
words, which batter
against the shutters
of a tired mind
then slip and lie,
disconsolate
in the dust
of memory.
These few escape.
But from your pen,
as verse slides free,
old words sing
a new song;
entwine, float,
dissolve, take fire;
in the darkness
they blaze then
die, leaving me
with the pleasure
of their afterglow.

Small Town in the Morning

1950 remembered

The music stirs
my memories.
I see it once again;
an empty street –
but for a mongrel
trotting home before
the sun steals
the hint of coolness
from the retreating dark.
Pepper trees hang
their leaves, scattering shade
upon a battered ute,
parked, abandoned
when the driver
staggered from the pub
last night.
Dust spirals sunwards,
drifts, filming the sky.
Shabby shops sag,
some boarded up
forsaken now,
while others struggle on.
A lone horseman
canters by, whistling
a counterpoint
to the magpie's song.

In the tiny park
the sun-bleached grass
is dry and crunches
underfoot.
The War Memorial,
with its wreaths
of wilting flowers
and lists of names –
so many names –
revives, renews
a small town's sorrow.
The Last Post sounds
in strident grief
for history
and a dying town.

Written after hearing a performance of 'Small Town' by Peter Sculthorpe

Hidden

The child hides,
peering out through
faded, aged eyes;
takes centre stage
in painful dreams
which linger,
stirring grief and fear.
From hidden depths
come drowning memories.
It speaks suddenly
forbidden words
in tones not ever heard
so long ago.
The child cries out
at last
for rescue and relief
but calls too late,
its hearers helpless now
to alter history.

Water

Water confined,
imprisoned, held quiet,
stagnant and slicked
with oily rainbows.

Water flowing free,
baptising rocks,
caressing weeds,
tickling sleeping trout
and trapping sunlight.

Water pouring through roads
and drowning fields,
sweeping the lanes
clear of fragile shacks
and people's lives.

In my rain-starved garden
as the country dries,
a shower barely
marks its passing
but on my outstretched hand
some tiny droplets glow
in the sunset light.

Listening

The sea sings
the same song
and whispers
the same words,
like sounds of time
passing unremembered
but with us still –
as we listen
to the sea's song
and try to understand
its whispers.
Ancestral memory
teases, fleeting,
gone as yet ungrasped.
So we listen
and wait, silent
beside a mystery;
waiting still
for understanding
of a language
as old as time.

The General

Like a Grecian mask
With empty eyes,
The old man's face
Wears the memory of beauty
Recorded in bone.
Nothing remains
Of the once-commanding soldier
But an elusive echo
To tease the observer
Into curiosity.
His shambling walk,
Pained incoherence
And heartbreaking bewilderment
Reveal only
His body's refusal
To follow his spirit
Into eternity.

Understood

It's fifty years ago
and yesterday.
The curtain between
what was then
and what is now
is porous, open weave.
The dark creeps through
but not the light.
It sometimes serves
its purpose, sometimes not.
Memories, charcoal grey,
crumble, sending motes
of that dark dust
floating through
to redden eyes
already tear-stained.
It needs an iron curtain
instead of scrim
to block the years of pain
remembering him.

The Long-case Clock

Clock ticking, tocking,
eating up the seconds
of my life,
winding them around
each spinning wheel,
in and out of gears,
twisting through springs,
slowing down that
measured tick, tock;
tick…tock, tick…tock
until the wheels stop spinning
and the gears are still
and in the silence
I too shall stop.
Will the world go on spinning
till all the clocks fall silent
and only the dust motes
spin and twist
in the empty air?

Runaway

Time is a runaway horse,
galloping out of control,
trundling the trap – and me –
helpless behind it.
The reins are flying loose,
the wheels spin in a spokeless blur,
there is no brake.
I clutch my seat,
praying I can hold on here
until we reach our destination,
wherever – and whenever –
that may be.
Whoa, horse, slow down!
I don't want to get there –
not yet! I'm in no hurry.
Let me enjoy the scenery
as I pass by; have time
to wave to friends or stop
to pass an hour or so
in pleasant company;
to think on what I see,
to write a line or two,
to simply stand and stare.
Whoa, horse, slow down!
The world will turn no faster
when I get there.

Carpe Diem

I close my book –
a novel about other people's lives
I read to escape my own;
to escape losing my husband,
to escape being lonely,
to escape losing my best friend,
to escape losing a beloved cat,
to escape being exhausted,
too tired to do the things
I really want to do,
To escape the fact
my tax return
remains undone!
To escape…to escape…
Oops! It hasn't worked.
Carpe diem! Seize the day!
I still have my life to live.
I stand up quickly –
but my back hurts
and my legs ache
and I'm tired, oh so tired.
I sit down slowly
and reopen my book.

What Did They Call Them?

Loud-mouthed 'patriots'
descendants of past refugees
who landed here
in days gone by,
decry the new arrivals,
call them 'terrorists'
who fled those, left behind
in multicoloured lands.
Ground into the winter
of rejection and abuse
which chills the heart,
those imports linger,
bravely steadfast.
Some come seeking
possibilities, haven.
They come in boats
above the unseen fishes.
In their fragile freedom
they float on a sea
of shimmering tears
that eddies up the shore
or flings itself
onto the jagged rocks –
without landfall.

Colour and song
come with them
as, wide-eyed and hopeful
they blossom if allowed
here on our indifferent soil,
giving life and beauty
to our grey-green lives,
though still despised by some.
What did they call them?

A Rueful Lament

written in 1972

I'm not too old –
Not old beyond recall!
I wear their clothes
And see – how on the ball
I am, how quick my wit.
(Not that they will
Even remember it.)
I sit and smile
At first and join their fun.
They talk of life and love
And the latest charity run.
But slowly my gaiety dims…
How dull my vaunted wit!
Of life and love?
They know not a jot of it.
For I am older than I thought –
Too old to be still young.
I've lived my life too long
While they have just begun.
I creep away; it's well
They notice not my going,
For youth has eyes for youth
And my disillusion's showing!

Thoughts on Pride and Prejudice

Mr Darcy?
What a pain!
Think he's classy?
Think again.
Turns his nose up
At Eliza –
Then he grows up
And desires her.
She in turn
Despising pride,
Makes his cheeks burn
With her snide
Remarks on his lack of tact.
He tells Liz
A fact's a fact!
Still, dear reader,
Don't despair.
He still wants her;
She does care.
So they wed
Despite her folks.
She has peer cred…
And Jane, her jokes.

The Moggy's Revenge

sung to the tune of 'The Wild Colonial Boy'

I am a wild colonial cat,
Black Bertie is me name.
Me feral mum and dad were shy
But I've a lust for fame.
I haunt the stage door
Day and night
I listen to them all;
Those songsters, musos, actor guys –
I'm sort of in their thrall.

One night a bloke
Made people laugh,
He sang a song so sad
For moggies all –
Both large and small –
It really made me mad.
He sang about
Poor Cousin Pat –
Or was it me cousin Pearl –
The words they stood
Me fur right up
And made me whiskers curl.

I cried me outrage
At his song,
I sobbed and shrieked me woe.
They slammed the door,
They had no heart –
They told me where to go.
But I followed him
From stage to pub,
I knew no shame or fear,
Then I sharpened me claws
On his bloody guitar
And I pissed into his beer.

This song is dedicated to Eric Bogle on behalf of moggies everywhere!

The Day After

Oh, I'm sunburnt,
Don't touch me!
I swam and I played,
I dug and I built
In the sand by the sea.
It was all great fun
But now –
Oh, I'm sunburnt,
Don't touch me!

I forgot my hat,
I forgot the time,
The sea was blue,
The hot sand fine.
I'll remember the day
And the sea
And the sand
But now –
Oh, I'm sunburnt,
Don't touch me!

Please go away,
Don't stand near me.
I'm red and I'm sore
And my nose is a mess;
My front's like a lobster
And my back's on fire.
Go away –
Oh, I'm sunburnt,
DON'T TOUCH ME!

Requiem for a Foolhardy *Pholcus Phalangoides*

with apologies to Dr Seuss

Fred was a spider, small and neat,
With spindly, gangling legs and feet.
He lived in a corner warm and dim,
He ignored me and I ignored him.

UNTIL

In the middle of the night, when the air was chill,
He did some acrobatics, just for a thrill,
Swinging high, swinging low on a thread so fine,
Till he was over a bed – and the bed was mine!
The warm air rising lured him down
To crawl on my forehead, ignoring the frown,
The jerk of my head, the unconscious twitch.
While I was deep in my slumbers, he tickled an itch.
So up came my hand to give it a scratch.
Fred tried to escape to a safe-seeming patch.
Still sleeping I roared out a triumphant snore…

But sadly and sorrowfully, Fred was no more.

www.ingramcontent.com/pod-product-compliance
Lightning Source LLC
Chambersburg PA
CBHW062147100526
44589CB00014B/1714